D1225070

12 ANCIENT
MYSTERIES

by M. J. York

STORY LIBRARY

www.12StoryLibrary.com

Copyright © 2017 by Peterson Publishing Company, North Mankato, MN 56003. All rights reserved. No part of this book may be reproduced or utilized in any form or by any means without written permission from the publisher.

12-Story Library is an imprint of Peterson Publishing Company and Press Room Editions.

Produced for 12-Story Library by Red Line Editorial

Photographs ©: Hung Chung Chih/Shutterstock Images, cover, 1; AP Images, 4; Jaroslav Moravcik/Shutterstock Images, 5, 28; Photos.com/Thinkstock, 6; Beth Swanson/Shutterstock Images, 7; Trazos sobre Papel/Shutterstock Images, 8; Holger Mette/iStockphoto, 10; centrill/iStockphoto, 11; Vladislav Gajic/Shutterstock Images, 12; Public Domain, 13, 19, 29; Dorothy Puray-Isidro/Shutterstock Images, 14; ArtMarie/iStockphoto, 16; jarnogz/iStockphoto, 17; Peter Vischer/Art Institute of Chicago/Detroit Publishing Company/Library of Congress, 18; GeorgiosArt/iStockphoto, 20; ZU_09/iStockphoto, 21; Bryan Busovicki/Shutterstock Images, 22; Leonard Zhukovsky/Shutterstock Images, 23; suronin/Shutterstock Images, 24, 25; duncan1890/iStockphoto, 26

Library of Congress Cataloging-in-Publication Data

Names: York, M. J., 1983-
Title: 12 ancient mysteries / by M.J. York.
Other titles: Twelve ancient mysteries
Description: North Mankato, MN : 12-Story Library, 2017. | Series: Scary and
  spooky | Audience: Grades 4 to 6. | Includes bibliographical references
  and index.
Identifiers: LCCN 2016002347 (print) | LCCN 2016011852 (ebook) | ISBN
  9781632352910 (library bound : alk. paper) | ISBN 9781632353412 (paperback
  : alk. paper) | ISBN 9781621434573 (hosted ebook)
Subjects: LCSH: Civilization, Ancient--Juvenile literature. |
  Antiquities--Juvenile literature. | Excavations (Archaeology)--Juvenile
  literature. | Curiosities and wonders--Juvenile literature.
Classification: LCC CB311 .Y67 2017 (print) | LCC CB311 (ebook) | DDC
  930.1--dc23
LC record available at http://lccn.loc.gov/2016002347

Printed in the United States of America
Mankato, MN
May, 2016

Access free, up-to-date content on this topic plus a full digital version of this book. Scan the QR code on page 31 or use your school's login at 12StoryLibrary.com.

Table of Contents

Excavators Die after Opening King Tut's Tomb

In 1922, Howard Carter and a team of excavators made a big find. It was one of the biggest finds in the history of Egyptology. They were digging in the Valley of the Kings. This area holds the tombs of many Egyptian pharaohs. They uncovered a tomb still filled with ancient treasure. This was a rare find. When Carter unsealed King Tutankhamen's tomb, he walked where no one had walked for more than 3,000 years.

But did he also unleash an ancient curse?

Less than one year after opening the tomb, the first person died. Lord Carnarvon had paid for the dig. Rumors said the lights went out in Cairo, Egypt, the moment he died. Other people connected to the excavation passed away one by one. The press went crazy for the story. Headlines declared the "curse of the Pharaoh." But Carnarvon was already sick before the tomb was opened.

Carter works in King Tut's tomb.

The mask found on Tutankhamen's mummy

The electricity went out in Cairo often. And the other deaths could be explained away. Only six of the 26 people who opened the tomb were dead within ten years. And Carter himself lived 17 more years. Was it a curse, or just a coincidence?

Many cultures believe it is unlucky to disturb the dead. Some think the ancient Egyptians had secret knowledge or magic. Written curses have been found protecting Egyptian burials. But King Tut's tomb did not have those. Some scientists guess that mummies might carry toxic mold. It could make people who handle the mummy sick or kill them. But no mold deaths have been proven. Regardless, cursed tombs, ancient spells, and mummies that come alive still haunt our movies and our dreams.

1323 BCE
Year King Tutankhamen died.

- Howard Carter opened King Tut's tomb in 1922.
- Several people involved in the excavation died in the following years.
- The ancient Egyptians sometimes included written curses with burials.
- Scientists believe that mummies can carry toxic mold.

THINK ABOUT IT

Do you believe in the curse of King Tut? Why might the press have exaggerated the story? Why might Howard Carter not try to stop the story?

Lost Island of Atlantis Escapes Searchers

An ancient story tells of the island of Atlantis. It was home to a civilization with advanced technology. But the Atlanteans grew greedy. The Greek gods did not like this. The island was swallowed up by the sea, killing the people. Some believe that the survivors of Atlantis scattered around the world. This would have spread their culture to other ancient civilizations. Searchers continue looking for the lost civilization. Many theories exist, but none have been proven.

The ancient Greek philosopher Plato wrote about Atlantis. His works are the only ancient sources that mention Atlantis. Plato described a large island in the Atlantic Ocean. It sank around 9600 BCE. Most historians read Plato's account as a myth or symbolic story.

Plato lived in ancient Greece.

Some people argue that Bimini Road is evidence for Atlantis.

People have proposed many locations for Atlantis. They compare clues from Plato's writings. One possibility is the Greek island of Santorini. It blew apart in a volcanic eruption around 1600 BCE. But if this was Atlantis, Plato was wrong about the date and the location. Tartessus in Spain and the island of Malta were both destroyed in ancient times. Either could lie behind the Atlantis story. Other Atlantis seekers have looked in the Bahamas. They point to an unusual underwater rock formation called Bimini Road. Searchers hope that new discoveries will shed light on this ancient mystery.

360 BCE

Year Plato wrote about Atlantis, more than 9,000 years after he said it was destroyed.

- Stories say the ancient Atlanteans had an advanced civilization before their island sank into the sea.
- Some people believe that the survivors may have spread around the world.
- Most historians believe Plato's Atlantis is a myth or a symbolic story.
- Explorers look for signs of Atlantis in Santorini in Greece, Tartessus in Spain, and other places around the world.

Stonehenge Watches Over English Plain

The ancient stone monument Stonehenge looms over the Salisbury Plain in southern England. People wonder how and why ancient people created the circles of giant stones. It was built and added to between 3000 and 1520 BCE.

Stonehenge has sparked legends for centuries.

No one is sure how the builders moved the giant stones. Some weigh as much as 45 tons (41 metric tons). Modern researchers have experimented with different methods, such as wooden rollers. But some do not believe the stones could move without modern technology. People have many theories. Some even suggest aliens helped.

200
Distance, in miles (320 km), that some of the stones were transported.

- Stonehenge consists of giant stones arranged in circles.
- No one is sure how or why the stone circles exist.
- Stone formations align with astronomical events, including sunrise on the summer solstice.
- The circle is part of a larger sacred landscape with other wooden and stone monuments.

There are even more theories about Stonehenge's meaning and purpose. Cremated bodies are buried there. Also, the stones align with the rising sun on the summer solstice and other astronomical events. Was the site a cemetery, a temple, a calendar, or all three? A series of excavations reveals Stonehenge is part of a larger sacred landscape. This includes additional stone and wood monuments and stretches across the plain. Archaeologists continue their work to uncover the region's secrets.

MERLIN AND STONEHENGE

A story from the 1100s uses magic to explain how Stonehenge was built. The author Geoffrey of Monmouth wrote about King Arthur. He explained that Arthur's magician Merlin put up the stones. In the story, the stones marked the mass grave of British noblemen killed in battle.

Silent Warriors Guard Emperor's Secret Tomb

In 1974, workers digging a well in China made an unbelievable find. They uncovered an ancient terra-cotta warrior statue. Archaeologists soon found a giant pit below ground. The pit had rows and rows of the statues. Each one had a unique face. Some of the statues were broken. The archaeologists reassembled the broken pieces. The warriors watch over the tomb of China's first emperor, Qin Shihuangdi. He ruled from 221 to 207 BCE. He united several kingdoms into his empire.

The statues were originally painted bright colors. They held

Thousands of terra-cotta statues were found in the pits.

real weapons. Archaeologists are studying how the statues were made. They reveal secrets of ancient Chinese technology. But Emperor Qin's greatest mystery is still waiting to be excavated. His tomb has not been disturbed in modern times. Scans of the ground show a huge underground palace complex. Ancient accounts say the tomb is a model of the empire. The rivers are said to flow with mercury, a poisonous liquid. The tomb had traps to kill robbers. No one

The statues guarding the tomb include horses.

knows whether the stories are true. Tests show high levels of mercury in the soil nearby. Archaeologists are waiting for better technology before they open the tomb. They want to protect the artifacts—and protect themselves from any deadly surprises.

8,000

Estimated number of unique terra-cotta warriors discovered guarding Emperor Qin's tomb.

- The warriors were discovered in 1974.
- Each terra-cotta warrior has a unique face.
- They were once painted and had real weapons.
- Emperor Qin's tomb has not been excavated and some of its contents are a mystery.

THE AFTERLIFE

Earlier Chinese kings believed human sacrifices would come with them to the afterlife. When they died, their ministers, wives, and people of the court were killed too. But Emperor Qin came to power after generations of war. The smaller population meant each person was more important to society. So Emperor Qin had his army and his attendants made from terra-cotta instead.

11

Mysterious Ancient City Flourished in North America

The ancient city of Cahokia is located in present-day Illinois. In 1150 CE, it had more residents than London, England. But the city was abandoned by around 1350. Other American Indian tribes lived in the region when Europeans first visited. They told no stories about the people who came before them.

Cahokia was a complex, well-planned city. Its 120 earthen mounds spread over 6 square miles (16 sq. km). An earth pyramid called Monks Mound was the largest mound in the Americas. The mound was 100 feet (30 m) tall. At its top was a building approximately 100 feet (30 m) long. The Cahokians controlled the surrounding countryside. They spread their culture as far north as Wisconsin.

People can visit the area where the ancient city of Cahokia was located.

20,000
Approximate population of Cahokia at its peak.

- The city of Cahokia was large and well planned and featured giant earthen mounds.
- Cahokia had the largest mound in the Americas.
- The population grew quickly.
- The people had no written language.

THINK ABOUT IT
What is the main idea of these two pages? List at least three pieces of evidence that support your choice.

Cahokia grew from a village into a large city over 250 years. Slowly, its people scattered and abandoned the site. They had no written language. They left no records or oral histories about what happened. Today, archaeologists suggest that a mix of drought, climate change, and war caused them to leave.

Monks Mound was the center of Cahokia.

THE MISSISSIPPIANS

Today, we call the culture that built Cahokia the Mississippians. We do not know what they called themselves. Cahokia is named for the people who lived in the region centuries after the city's fall. The Mississippians began farming across the region before 1000. They gathered into villages and later cities. They built giant mounds of earth, mostly for religious purposes. Modern descendants include the Natchez tribe of Mississippi.

13

The Great Pyramid Hides Many Mysteries

The Great Pyramid is at least 4,500 years old. It is the largest and oldest of the three pyramids of Giza, Egypt. Experts agree it belongs to Pharaoh Khufu. Archaeologists have studied it closely. But it still has many secrets.

One of the biggest mysteries is how the pyramid was built. The simplest theory is that workers hauled the stone blocks up external ramps. But no one has found evidence of a ramp. Another theory says the ramp spiraled around on the inside of the pyramid. Small rooms inside the pyramid with no other clear purpose might support this theory.

Others question how an ancient civilization could have accomplished building such a large structure. Carving and moving the stones with no modern tools seems almost impossible. The pyramid's measurements show exact

The Great Pyramid is one of the largest structures ever built.

THE SPHINX

Near the pyramids sits the Great Sphinx. The giant statue has the body of a lion and the head of a man. Some believe the weathering of the stone shows that the statue is between 7,000 and 10,000 years old. But most experts say Khufu's son Khafre built it. Mysterious tunnels seem to lead under the Sphinx. No one has explored them in case it damages the statue. It is unclear what may be hidden under the mysterious monument.

calculations. The pyramid also aligns with points on Earth and in the stars. Is this a coincidence? If not, how did the Egyptians build so precisely? Some note that pyramids were built around the world. But these cultures are supposed to have had no contact with each other. Why is the pyramid so universal? Some say a lost advanced civilization such as Atlantis or even aliens built the pyramids.

In addition, the Great Pyramid has many hidden doors and chambers. It has closed shafts that are not found in other pyramids. It also has mysterious empty spaces. These all spark a variety of theories about their purposes. The debate goes on among both Egyptologists and fringe theorists.

2.3 million
Approximate number of blocks used to build the Great Pyramid.

- The Great Pyramid is one of the largest structures ever built.
- Workers likely hauled stones up ramps to build the pyramid, but no one knows exactly how they did it.
- The pyramid seems to show precise calculations and aligns with the stars and Earth.
- The purpose of mysterious rooms, passages, and doors in the pyramid are debated.

Nazca Lines Draw Patterns across the Desert

More than 1,000 giant line drawings crisscross the desert in southern Peru. Many are several hundred feet long. Most of the lines were complete by 500 AD. Some are even older. It is hard to find the lines on the ground. It is even harder to understand their patterns. They are easier to see from the air because they are so large. The patterns are animals, plants, and shapes.

No one knows what the mysterious figures mean.

Some people believe the lines could be landing strips for alien aircraft.

The Nazca removed the top layer of stones from the desert floor to make the lines. This exposed the lighter-colored sand beneath. The lines hardened because they are in one of the driest and least windy places on Earth. People marvel at the longest lines. They run almost perfectly straight for up to 30 miles (48 km). Some believe the Nazca would have needed to see the lines from the air to create them so precisely. But modern volunteers have proved it is possible from the ground. They used string to guide them.

It is a mystery why the Nazca created patterns they could not see clearly. Some researchers thought they were a calendar linked to the movement of the stars. But astronomers found no relationship. Some people believe the lines are a message for aliens. The most recent studies suggest the Nazca held processions along the lines. Researchers think the religious ceremonies might have been about water. But it is likely we will never know for sure.

935
Length, in feet (285 m), of a Nazca figure of a pelican.

- The lines in the desert show animals, plants, and symbols, as well as straight lines that run for miles.
- The Nazca created the lines by removing stones from the desert floor to expose lighter-colored sand.
- The lines are best seen from the sky.
- No one knows for sure why the Nazca created the lines.

Historians Seek Evidence of Legendary King Arthur

Legends tell of King Arthur, who lived in the 500s. He led the Britons in a war against the Saxon invaders. Later tales such as *The Death of Arthur* tell about his life. They describe the Knights of the Round Table in Arthur's castle, Camelot. They tell of the sorcerer Merlin and the quest for the Holy Grail. But was there a real King Arthur?

Archaeologists seek clues about Arthur in places named in the legends. They excavate unnamed forts from Arthur's time. Sometimes inscriptions or other artifacts hint at Arthur. People still hope to find Camelot or prove that an existing site is the lost castle. But no one has proven a link to the king.

Historians look for evidence in written documents. Gildas was a monk who wrote about the Battle of Badon. Legends say the king led the troops there. Gildas did not mention Arthur by name. But the monk did not name a different leader, either. Was he writing about Arthur? The historian Nennius first mentioned Arthur by name. He wrote about Arthur in the 800s. But we cannot be sure if Nennius is recording history or legend. Lost manuscripts may have better proof.

Much is unknown about King Arthur.

ARTUR KÖNIG
V. ENGLAND

The Knights of the Round Table is one of the legends surrounding King Arthur.

The name *Arthur* means "bear." It is possible it was a leader's title and not a name at all. Several Roman war leaders could have been Arthur. Or he could be mythological. Unless we find better evidence underground or discover an unknown manuscript, we may never know.

1485

Year *The Death of Arthur* was published, almost 1,000 years after Arthur's time.

- King Arthur is said to have lived during the 500s.
- No known sources written during Arthur's life mention him by name.
- Many archaeological sites and artifacts are linked to the king, but nothing is proven.
- A historical Arthur could be a combination of several Roman war leaders.

A SCOTTISH ARTHUR?

Another theory suggests a real Scottish prince named Arthur was the Arthur of legend. He lived at the end of the 500s. He was the son of King Aidan of Scotland. Believers say the earliest historical sources about King Arthur match recorded details of this Arthur's life. They also note that the Scottish Arthur's historical battles and allies correspond to the legends.

Ancient Seafarers May Have Reached the Americas

Explorers Christopher Columbus and Leif Eriksson both came to the Americas. Evidence hints that others might have reached the continents earlier.

Stories say Saint Brendan the Navigator of Ireland sailed west in the 560s. Some things he saw match up with real features and life found on the way to the Americas. The Welsh say Prince Madoc sailed the Atlantic Ocean around 1170. Stories say his followers married members of American Indian tribes. Later European explorers told of finding American Indians with light skin and blue eyes. Legends are slim evidence to prove early European contact. But people did not used to believe Viking stories of the New World. Now we have found their settlements and know their stories were true. Is there truth behind these legends as well?

The Phoenicians were powerful seafarers. Their boats were likely advanced enough to cross the Atlantic Ocean. But did they? Believers point to coins found scattered around the Americas. They say the

Columbus was one of the first European explorers to reach the Americas.

The Phoenicians dominated the Mediterranean Sea from the 800s to the 500s BCE.

Phoenicians left them. Skeptics question why no other evidence has turned up. They think the coins are hoaxes. Or maybe they were misinterpreted.

Polynesians spent hundreds of years sailing the Pacific Ocean. They colonized tiny islands. But did they reach South America? Some evidence says yes. South American crops such as the sweet potato came to Polynesia before the time of Columbus. Chicken bones found in South America could be evidence, if their radiocarbon dating is correct. DNA testing of modern populations from 2014 is the strongest evidence so far. It suggests Polynesians from Easter Island had early contact with South Americans. However, skeptics are waiting for DNA evidence from ancient bones to close the case.

10
Percent of modern Easter Islanders' DNA that is American Indian.

- It is said that Saint Brendan the Navigator of Ireland sailed west in the 560s.
- The Welsh say Prince Madoc sailed the Atlantic Ocean around 1170.
- Other cultures are said to have traveled to the Americas early as well.
- DNA analysis can help prove contact among ancient peoples.

Mysterious Statues Guard Easter Island

Easter Island is one of the most isolated places on Earth. It is 1,200 miles (1,900 km) from its nearest neighbor in the Pacific Ocean. And it is 2,000 miles (3,200 km) from the coast of South America. Yet it was home to a cultured society called the Rapa Nui. They created hundreds of giant stone statues called Moai.

On average, the statues are 13 feet (4 m) tall. They weigh 13 tons (12 metric tons). Some were much bigger. Researchers believe the Moai represent people or gods. But no one knows. Nor do we know how the Rapa Nui moved the statues. Oral histories say the statues walked into place. Modern experiments have tested this idea. They moved an upright statue by rocking it back and forth. But the statues also could have been dragged or moved by log rollers.

The Moai are believed to be the spirits of ancestors or chiefs.

The biggest mystery of Easter Island is what happened to its climate and people. When people first came to the island, it was forested and had many birds. Experts date the settlement from 400 to 1200. But when Europeans first visited the island in the 1700s, the land was barren. The old theory was that the islanders cut down the trees to move the Moai. This ruined the island's ecology. There was starvation. The population dropped from 20,000 to 3,000. New theories say the population was never that high. It dropped after Europeans introduced diseases and slavery. Causes of deforestation could be the rats that came in the first islanders' boats or climate change. The mystery remains unsolved.

887

Number of Moai on Easter Island, including those still unfinished in quarries.

- Easter Island is isolated in the Pacific Ocean.
- The Moai might represent people or gods.
- Researchers do not know exactly how the islanders moved the giant stone figures.
- The population and ecology of Easter Island seem to have collapsed, but no one is certain why.

It is unclear exactly how the Moai statues were moved.

Long-Lost Indus Civilization Hides Many Secrets

The ancient Indus Civilization grew from 2500 to 1700 BCE in modern Pakistan. It was larger than ancient Egypt or Mesopotamia. Yet no one knew it existed until the 1920s. Then two large cities, Harappa and Mohenjo Daro, were uncovered. Much is still unknown.

Archaeologists found advanced technology and organization at the sites. Mohenjo Daro is laid out similar to a modern city. It has a sewer system. Its buildings have plumbing. But no one knows how its government worked. The most impressive public building is called the Great Bath. It may have been used for religious ceremonies. The Great Bath suggests the citizens' religion focused on cleanliness.

It is clear the citizens of Mohenjo Daro were wealthy.

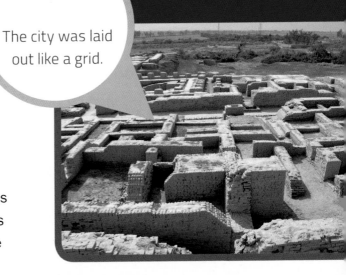

Today we know very little because we cannot read Indus writing.

Archaeologists once believed Mohenjo Daro fell because it was conquered. Bodies in the streets looked as if they were left where they died. But further research shows the bodies came from different times. The theory does not add up. Explanations of disease or flooding are unproven. A slower culture change as groups of people moved in and out of the area seems most likely. However, some fringe theorists believe an ancient deadly weapon is to blame. They say some bricks in the city turned to glass. This could happen only at a very high temperature. They say the *Mahabharata*, an ancient Indian poem, describes the weapon.

Others counter this theory. They say the high temperatures can happen in natural fires. They ask why any walls are still standing if a powerful weapon hit the city. They say the poem was misinterpreted. We may never know what happened.

250
Approximate area, in acres (100 ha), of Mohenjo Daro.

- The Indus Civilization was forgotten until the 1920s.
- The city of Mohenjo Daro had advanced technology, but we cannot read its writing.
- Researchers have found a sewer system and impressive buildings.
- No one knows why the civilization fell.

THINK ABOUT IT

Brainstorm two or three things you would like to know about the Indus Civilization. Using books or the Internet, research answers to your questions.

25

Ancient Labyrinth Still Baffles Researchers

Ancient Greek myths tell of the labyrinth of King Minos of Crete. At the center of the labyrinth lived the Minotaur. This monster had the body of a man and the head of a bull. King Minos sacrificed young men and women to the monster. Finally, the hero Theseus found his way through the maze. Minos's daughter Ariadne helped him. Theseus killed the Minotaur and stopped the

An illustration of King Minos

1300 BCE

Year by which the palace at Knossos was abandoned.

- Greek myths tell the story of the labyrinth of Crete and the monster within.
- Theseus made it through the labyrinth and killed the Minotaur.
- Archaeologists debate the location of the labyrinth and whether it existed.
- The palace at Knossos and its artwork featuring bulls could inspire the myths.

SYMBOLIC LABYRINTHS

The labyrinth is a common symbol in many cultures. Stone carvings of labyrinths in Europe could date back thousands of years. The ancient Egyptians built a huge labyrinth at Hawara. Labyrinth symbols appear in Christian churches and on American Indian baskets. Labyrinths often represent a journey inward. Or they can be paths toward salvation or gaining spiritual knowledge.

sacrifices. Is this story a myth, or is there some truth behind it?

Ancient sources say the labyrinth was located at Knossos on Crete. Archaeologists uncovered a large palace there. It has complex corridors. It has artwork featuring bulls. Many say the real palace inspired the mythological labyrinth. Ancient Roman authors wrote down Greek legends centuries later. They believed the labyrinth was a nearby cave complex instead. Some modern researchers agree. But skeptics say the cave was an ancient quarry. Ancient coins show the labyrinth and the Minotaur. But do they illustrate a myth or real history?

Bulls were important in ancient Crete's religion. A fresco at Knossos from 1400 BCE shows a boy leaping over a bull. Bull leaping might have been a religious ceremony. It might have been a sport or competition. Or the fresco might be symbolic, and no one leaped over bulls. Bulls are everywhere in ancient Crete's art.

Fact Sheet

- As time passes, civilizations fall. Records are lost. Languages are no longer spoken. Buildings collapse and are buried. The past hides many secrets.

- Myths and other stories hint at past events. But it is hard to know which parts are true and which were elaborated on over time. Other myths are symbolic and deal with aspects of religion or society. They are not meant to tell about real events.

- Historians find traces of the past in ancient writings and in manuscripts. Archaeologists dig up sites and find buildings and artifacts. But this evidence is hard to interpret. Experts often have different theories about what the evidence means.

- Experts and other theorists look at the evidence. They put together clues to support their theories about the past. Often there are multiple ways to look at the clues. It is difficult to prove that a given theory is the correct answer. Many ancient mysteries will remain unsolvable unless we find new evidence.

- Some types of evidence are considered more reliable than others. Inscriptions or small objects found alone are not trustworthy. Finding artifacts together with other evidence is important. Scientific techniques such as radiocarbon dating and DNA testing are considered more solid. But even these can be inaccurate.

Glossary

align
To line up.

court
A ruler's group of advisers and nobles.

cremate
To burn a body after death.

Egyptology
The study of ancient Egypt.

excavator
A person who digs up artifacts and other things left from the past.

fringe theorist
A person who holds a belief with which only a small group of people agree.

inscription
Words or symbols cut into rock or another surface.

labyrinth
A maze.

manuscript
A handwritten document.

radiocarbon dating
A method for dating an artifact by analyzing its atoms of carbon.

solstice
The longest or shortest day of the year.

terra-cotta
A brownish orange clay.

For More Information

Books

Aronson, Marc, and Mike Parker Pearson. *If Stones Could Speak: Unlocking the Secrets of Stonehenge.* Washington, DC: National Geographic, 2010.

Civilizations: The History of the Ancient World. London: TickTock, 2009.

Hart, George. *Ancient Egypt.* New York: DK, 2014.

Visit 12StoryLibrary.com

Scan the code or use your school's login at **12StoryLibrary.com** for recent updates about this topic and a full digital version of this book. Enjoy free access to:

- Digital ebook
- Breaking news updates
- Live content feeds
- Videos, interactive maps, and graphics
- Additional web resources

Note to educators: Visit 12StoryLibrary.com/register to sign up for free premium website access. Enjoy live content plus a full digital version of every 12-Story Library book you own for every student at your school.

Index

About the Author

M. J. York is a children's author
and editor. She has always been
fascinated with ancient mysteries
and legends, including King Arthur,
Stonehenge, and Atlantis. She lives in
Minnesota with her family.

**READ MORE FROM
12-STORY LIBRARY**

Every 12-Story Library book
is available in many formats.
For more information, visit
12StoryLibrary.com.